RESOLUTE

RESOLUTE

FOUNDATIONS FOR MEN

RESOLUTE: Foundations For Men
Published by RESOLUTE
Author Vince Miller

Interior Design by Vince Miller
Interior Layout by Gretchen Miller
Cover Design and Layout by Eric Beavers
Printed by Ideal Printers

ISBN: 978-0-9982133-3-0

Printed in the United States of America

RESOLUTE

TABLE OF CONTENTS

RESOLUTE

HOW TO USE THIS HANDBOOK

USE THIS HANDBOOK WITH OUR STREAMING VIDEOS.

As you navigate this guide, you will see that the lesson was designed for use with online streaming videos viewable only with a membership on our website at www.beresolute.org. The videos are what you will use to lead a group of men. Each lesson corresponds to a video. The best part is Vince Miller, our founder, has structured the streaming videos in such a way that they lead the time, so you don't have to. You do not have to prepare hours of content – he does it for you. If you are "hosting," all you need to do is push play and pause at the appropriate time and reference the content in the handbook.

ABOUT THE RESOLUTE METHOD.

At Resolute we provide you with a game plan. We are not just giving you content, but a method field-tested with hundreds of men. While the content is crucial, it is the method that is essential to spiritual change in a man's life. Each session has components we have tested that produce results in a man's life. In each lesson, you will notice clear goals and outcomes, purposeful discussion with other men, a rich study of God's Word, practical application, and a positive focus for 60-90 minutes. While we know, men enjoy our content; we hope this commitment to method deepens their relationship with Christ and one another.

THERE IS MORE CONTENT.

The series is not all the content you have access to with a membership. Also, we have stand-alone volumes to compliment this set. Check it out online. Or reach out to us at info@beresolute.org.

RESOLUTE

GETTING STARTED

The Resolute Directional Experience is designed to be a comprehensive discipleship plan for men. We have field-tested the Resolute method with hundreds of men over the last decade. It is intended to help men spiritually mature and has yielded proven results. Our program boasts of a complex logic model that is behavior-based and designed to nurture spiritual transformation for men through God's Word.

TO EFFECTIVELY USE THIS HANDBOOK

ONE | GATHER A TEAM.

Assembling a team is key. A team should include a pair of leaders who become the "On-Site Hosts" for the experience. We believe working in pairs is by far the most practical approach. Remember every Maverick needs a Goose.

TWO | RECRUIT MEN.

Don't stress. Whether you recruit half a dozen men or a hundred, the content will work efficiently. When recruiting, we have found the greatest success is finding men who are hungry to grow spiritually. While the content is good for any believer of any age, the best recruit is the one who wants to be there. These are what we call "hungry" men. To be clear these are men who hunger for the Word of God, and occasionally some food as well!

THREE | ENSURE EACH MAN HAS A HANDBOOK.

All our guides are purchased online at www.beresolute.org in the store. These are your guides for taking notes, guiding a dialogue with men in your group, and recording outcomes at the end of every lesson. Handbooks also include other materials for additional development. You will want one for each lesson series.

FOUR | LEADER ONLINE ENGAGEMENT.

If you are a leader and have purchased an online membership, you can view all the material. You will be able to listen to audio recaps, watch the videos, read the full transcripts, and even review past lessons.

FIVE | ACCESS MORE MATERIAL & RESOLUTE STAFF.

At Resolute we are not just selling curriculum. We are inviting you into an experience. Here are other tools for you to utilize.

- Men's Daily Devotionals.
- Men's Weekly Audio Podcasts.

You can also invite a representative from the Resolute to speak at your:

- Men's Group.
- Men's Retreat.
- Men's Breakfast.

It is our goal to partner with you and your men's ministry. We want to resource you with tools that compliment your development as a man of God and a leader.

SIX | CONNECT SOCIALLY.

We would love to have you join our social networks. Head to our home page www.beresolute.org and connect with us on Twitter, LinkedIn, and Facebook.

RESOLUTE

THE PRESENTER/AUTHOR

Vince Miller grew up on the west coast and was born in Vallejo, California where he spent all his childhood. At age 20, he made a profession of faith while in college and felt a sudden and strong call to work in full-time ministry. After college and graduate school, he invested two decades working with notable ministries like Young Life, InterVarsity Christian Fellowship, the local church, and in Senior Interim roles many times. He lives in St. Paul, Minnesota with Christina, his wife, and their three teenage children.

In March of 2014, he founded Resolute out of his passion for the discipleship and leadership development of men. This passion was born out of his own personal need for growth. Vince would say that he turned everywhere to find a man who would mentor, disciple, and develop him and over the course of his spiritual life and that he often received two answers from well-meaning Christian leaders – "Either they did not know what to do in a mentoring relationship, or they simply did not have the time to do it." Vince learned that he was not alone, and that many Christian men were seeking this type of mentorship relationship with another man. Out of this he felt compelled to build an organization that would focus on one thing, ensuring that men who want to be discipled have the opportunity, and that they can have real tools to disciple other men.

Vince is an authentic and transparent leader who loves to communicate to men and has a deep passion for God's Word. He has authored two books, The Generous Life and his newest book Convictions, which helps men understand how to close the gap between feeling convicted and living with conviction. And he is primary content creator of all Resolute content and training materials.

A PERSONAL NOTE FROM VINCE

I pray this experience will benefit your life and your spiritual journey as a man. I have three things that I hope you will do as you engage. First, that you will be receptive to the Word of God. I love, that we dig into the Bible every time we meet. The Bible is not an afterthought in Resolute – it is the means of discovering God and transformation. Second, lean into the brotherhood of this experience. Build friendships, share transparently, and have conversations that go beyond the superficial. Third, apply what you have learned. Take an action item with you every week, knowing that one small step weekly leads to success over a lifetime.

Keep moving forward,

DISCIPLESHIP

THE INDUCTIVE METHOD

OBSERVATION. EXPLORE THE TEXT TAKING SPECIAL NOTE OF...

- **WORDS**: Look for repeated words as well as the specific terms used to describe people, places, and things.
- **CHARACTERS**: Their roles and actions within the text.
- **GRAMMAR**: Identify the subject, verb, and object of each sentence. What verbs represent the text or take center stage? Look for the use of contrasts and comparisons used to make or emphasize a central point.
- **STRUCTURE**: Examine how sentences and paragraphs come together, paying special attention to transitions and connection terms like "therefore."
- **GENRE**: Discern the genre of the text, whether poetry, prose, a letter, a prophetic, or narrative style.
- **MOOD**: Notice the tone of the text by paying attention to actions, emotions, and/or challenges.

SMALL GROUP QUESTIONS:

- Name.
- What you do for a living.
- Who is in your immediate family.
- Where you live.

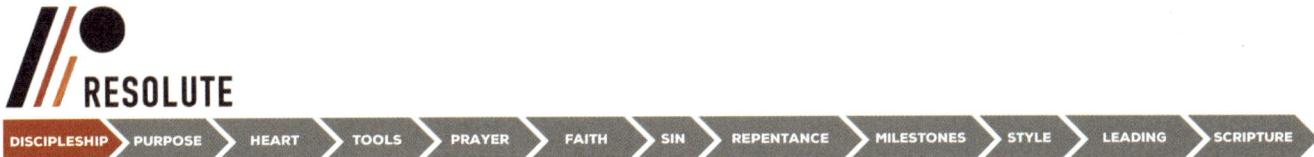

RESOLUTE

INTERPRETATION. FIND THE AUTHOR'S INTENDED MEANING TO THE ORIGINAL AUDIENCE.

TO DO:

- Ask reporter style questions from direct observation of the text. Who? What? Where? When? How? Why?
- While studying, keep in mind your own cultural and personal assumptions and biases.
- Determine the author's main point. Even though a text will contain numerous possibilities, usually one theme surfaces.
- Determine and focus on that one overarching point.

ADDITIONAL:

- Always lay aside preconceived ideas and speculations while doing the inductive side of the study and consider how the text connects to the life of Jesus.

PERSONAL APPLICATION. HOW THIS APPLIES TO MY LIFE TODAY.

- How does this text apply to my life? What changes do I need to make?
- How does this observation and interpretation impact my core relationships, i.e. with God and others?
- When applied to my life, how would the text change my worldview (how I think), actions (what I do), and identity (Who I am)?

THE WISE & FOOLISH BUILDERS

24 "Everyone then who hears these words of mine and does them will be like a wise man who
built his house on the rock. 25 And the rain fell, and the floods came, and the winds blew and
beat on that house, but it did not fall, because it had been founded on the rock. 26 And everyone who hears these words of mine and does not do them will be like a foolish man who built
his house on the sand. 27 And the rain fell, and the floods came, and the winds blew and beat
against that house, and it fell, and great was the fall of it."

28 And when Jesus finished these sayings, the
crowds were astonished at his teaching, 29 for he
was teaching them as one who had authority, and
not as their scribes.

MATTHEW 7:24-29, ESV

MY ACTION ITEMS:

Issues to Address. Steps to Take.

How can I become a wise person? What area of my life needs more integration?

CHECK OUT THE BLOG: beresolute.org/foundation

RESOLUTE

RESOLUTE EXPECTATIONS

Discussion Rule: MANAGE YOUR CONVERSATION

- Everyone participates, no individual dominates.
- Silence confers agreement.
- Actively listen to understand the materials and others' perspectives.
- Do not interrupt others. Let men complete their thoughts and ask clarifying questions.
- When you disagree, do so respectfully. Consider using statements like, "I would like to push back on that," or "I respectfully disagree."
- Speak to the topic at hand. Discipline your mind and words.

Personal Rule: MANAGE YOURSELF

- Expect challenge and tension.
- Show up and be present. Monitor your use of electronic devices.
- Communicate when you are unable to attend.
- Be willing to be held accountable.
- Be willing to accept and admit when you are wrong.
- Be transparent and authentic.

Confidentiality Rule: MANAGE CONFIDENTIALITY

- What is shared in the group stays in the room.
- Your wife needs to know you, not other members. (But feel free to share your positive feelings about the group).

Focus Rule: MANAGE TIMELINESS

- Respect the agenda by staying on topic and not digressing.
- Stay engaged by writing down stray or off topic thoughts.
- Be present and ready to start and end on time.

Spirituality Rule: MANAGE YOUR DISCIPLINE

- Read your Bible regularly. Bring your Bible or Bible application to group time.
- Pray daily.
- Take responsibility for your spiritual health and growth.

Action Rule: APPLY WHAT YOU LEARN

- Establish an action item for yourself each week.
- Take notes your way, and practice this as a pattern.
- Participate in discussion.

THE PURPOSE OF MAN

SMALL GROUP QUESTIONS:

- Introduce yourself and share a little about your family.
- Briefly discuss the specifics of your work, like your title, general responsibilities, etc.
- Answer the question, "What is the purpose of your work?"

THE BEGINNING

8 Now the Lord God had planted a garden in the east, in Eden; and there he put the man he
had formed. 9 The Lord God made all kinds of trees grow out of the ground—trees that were
pleasing to the eye and good for food. In the middle of the garden were the tree of life and
the tree of the knowledge of good and evil.

10 A river watering the garden flowed from Eden; from there it was separated into four head-
waters. 11 The name of the first is the Pishon; it winds through the entire land of Havilah, where
there is gold. 12 (The gold of that land is good; aromatic resin and onyx are also there.) 13 The
name of the second river is the Gihon; it winds through the entire land of Cush. 14 The name of
the third river is the Tigris; it runs along the east side of Ashur. And the fourth river is the Eu-
phrates.

15 The Lord God took the man and put him in the Garden of Eden to work it and take care of it.
16 And the Lord God commanded the man, "You are free to eat from any tree in the garden; 17
but you must not eat from the tree of the knowledge of good and evil, for when you eat from
it you will certainly die." 18 The Lord God said, "It is not good for the man to be alone. I will make
a helper suitable for him."

19 Now the Lord God had formed out of the ground all the wild animals and all the birds in the
sky. He brought them to the man to see what he would name them; and whatever the man
called each living creature, that was its name. 20 So the man gave names to all the livestock,
the birds in the sky and all the wild animals.

CONTINUED ON THE NEXT PAGE

But for Adam no suitable helper was found. 21 So the Lord God caused the man to fall into a
deep sleep; and while he was sleeping, he took one of the man's ribs and then closed up the
place with flesh. 22 Then the Lord God made a woman from the rib he had taken out of the
man, and he brought her to the man.

23 The man said, "This is now bone of my bones and flesh of my flesh; she shall be called
'woman,' for she was taken out of man." 24 That is why a man leaves his father and mother
and is united to his wife, and they become one flesh.

25 Adam and his wife were both naked, and they felt no shame.

GENESIS 2:8-25

MY ACTION ITEMS:

Issues to Address. Steps to Take.

What issue do I need to address to become the man and leader God designed me to be? What steps do I need to take this week to live this out?

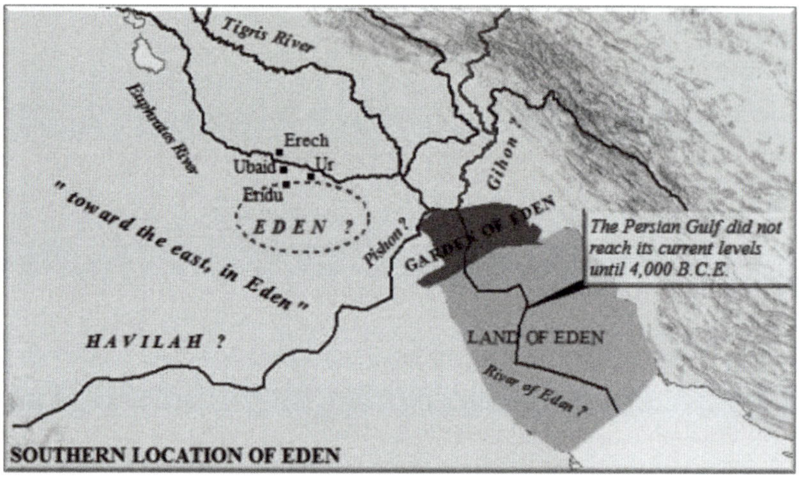

SOUTHERN LOCATION OF EDEN

SKILL DEVELOPMENT // TIME WITH GOD

Find a time of the day that you could spend 30 min. with God. Choose 5 days of the week that will work using your 30-minute time slot.

RESOLUTE

VALUES | CODE OF CONDUCT

The following core values drive the RESOLUTE program. When internalized, these core values impact the external behavior of the organization and its members. RESOLUTE relies on these values as a plumb line for its products, processes, and programs. Therefore, RESOLUTE men agree to uphold our CORE VALUES as a CODE OF CONDUCT. We require members to agree to the following and to renew their agreement annually.

DISCIPLESHIP

We value and actively embrace discipleship. This life-long process originates with profession of faith in Jesus Christ and continues by learning the truth taught throughout the Bible and reinforced by life-on-life experiences. We honor Jesus' method of developing his disciples while walking side-by-side with them.

LEADERSHIP

We value leadership and believe every man leads within his unique context. Men lead by exerting influence in appropriate and truthful ways. We know we are leading effectively when we look behind us to discover others following. Some will lead hundreds, others a few, each according to his own calling from God. We value ensuring that men understand this responsibility and that they demonstrate it to a world desperate for leaders.

ACCOUNTABILITY

We value personal accountability. Since the dawn of time man has craved the freedom to make independent decisions from God. However, this stance leads to spiritual, emotional, relational, and sometimes physical decay. The Bible calls these choices and activities "sin." By embracing responsibility for the consequences of one's actions and decisions, we set a godly example and avoid even the smallest appearance of impropriety.

TRUTH

We pursue truth as witnessed in the Bible through the life of Jesus Christ. He alone is "the way, the truth, and the life" (John 14:6) providing the plumb line for all we can be, know, and do. We live in a world full of deception that is provoked by and often hostile to this truth. We will give our lives for it, remembering that at the end of our lives we will stand before the throne of our holy God. We will do everything to apply this certainty to our lives regardless of how we feel, listening to truth over our desires. We will impart truth in our work life, family life, and to future generations knowing that we're sharing the one true hope of the world.

SELFLESSNESS

We value the welfare of our neighbors and Christ over self. When we accept God's offer of salvation through Jesus Christ who gave his life for us, we abdicate our plans, pride, and right to be king of our lives. Then we accept our two core duties – to love God and to love others. This calling to a selfless life is practiced daily as we choose the welfare of others over our own when pride, arrogance, and self-protections rear their ugly heads.

INTEGRATED INTEGRITY

We value integrity. This means we will be honest, transparent, and authentic in all interactions with others, whether in work, business or at home. When we integrate godly values at the deepest level of our core, we become men of integrity. We live authentic lives by speaking up, standing up, and refusing to hide our sin. The lifelong challenge of integrity for men who can easily compartmentalize their lives and become disintegrated can lead to a humbling road of discovery. The integrated man lives with resolve, knowing he has nothing to hide from others, himself, and God, and is willing to be put to the test.

FEARLESS PURSUIT OF GOD

We value living fearless lives. Human fear stands in direct opposition to faith, so living fearfully during this temporary life is not the calling of God's man. We understand that reverent and holy fear of God alone is not conditional. We value holy fear in that it keeps us humble and living in obedience to God alone. Courage is required to live fearless of anything or anyone but God because we know that living in this manner could cost what we do not want to lose. It's worth it because healthy fear of God is the beginning of wisdom and reward.

LAUNCHING

We value discipling, developing, and launching men into the world. We emphasize becoming a launching pad rather than a landing point. We envision our end product as men entering the world and changing it for the better. And they cannot do this without being launched into the world.

RECEPTIVITY OF THE HEART

[4] And when a great crowd was gathering and people from town after town came to him, he said in a
parable, [5] "A sower went out to sow his seed. And
as he sowed, some fell along the path and was
trampled underfoot, and the birds of the air de-
voured it. [6] And some fell on the rock, and as it grew
up, it withered away, because it had no mois-
ture. [7] And some fell among thorns, and the thorns
grew up with it and choked it. [8] And some fell into
good soil and grew and yielded a hundredfold." As
he said these things, he called out, "He who has
ears to hear, let him hear."

[9] And when his disciples asked him what this para-
ble meant, [10] he said, "To you it has been given to know the secrets of the kingdom of God, but
for others they are in parables, so that 'seeing they may not see, and hearing they may not
understand.' [11] Now the parable is this: The seed is the word of God. [12] The ones along the path
are those who have heard; then the devil comes and takes away the word from their hearts,
so that they may not believe and be saved. [13] And the ones on the rock are those who, when
they hear the word, receive it with joy. But these have no root; they believe for a while, and in
time of testing fall away. [14] And as for what fell among the thorns, they are those who hear,
but as they go on their way they are choked by the cares and riches and pleasures of life, and
their fruit does not mature. [15] As for that in the good soil, they are those who, hearing the
word, hold it fast in an honest and good heart, and bear fruit with patience.

LUKE 8:4-15

MY ACTION ITEMS:

Issues to Address. Steps to Take.

Which soil represents you currently? What steps do you need to take to address this?

Take the Resolute Assessment on the back.

SMALL GROUP DISCUSSION

- Introduce yourself.
- What is the one thing you had to do last week that you simply did not want to do?
- What about the task (or you) made it difficult or objectionable?

SKILL DEVELOPMENT // TIME WITH GOD

Choose a location and environment that works well for you (quiet, free from distraction, somewhere you enjoy).

RESOLUTE

TWO ASSESSMENTS

FIRST ASSESSMENT: YOU COMPLETE

This assessment is an overly simplified 360 tool that invites personal assessment with three opened-ended questions. Specifically, what do you need to **keep**, **start**, and **stop** doing. Please take a few minutes right now to reflect and complete the following questions.

1. What one thing that I need to **STOP** doing to be a better disciple of Jesus Christ?

2. What one thing that I need to **KEEP** doing to be a better disciple of Jesus Christ?

3. What one thing that I need to **START** doing to be a better disciple of Jesus Christ?

SECOND ASSESSMENT: SOMEONE ELSE COMPLETES

We are also asking that you give this assessment to someone else. This assessment can be given to a spouse, friend, employee of your choosing. The following represents text that you can email to a few people of your choosing.

Hey <insert friends name>

Over the next year I am participating in a program called Resolute (www.beresolute.org), which is a Christian leadership program for men. As a part of my time I am asking others who know to me, to give me feedback so that I can become a better father, husband, and leader. Would you take 5 minutes to complete these three questions below and return them to me? I would like for you to be honest and thoughtful, as I do want to grow in my leadership and faith. I am hoping your answers will help me to identify some ways I can leverage my strengths and manage my weaknesses.

- What one thing does this Resolute member need to **STOP** doing to be a better disciple of Jesus Christ?
- What one thing does this Resolute member need to **KEEP** doing to be a better disciple of Jesus Christ?
- What one thing does this Resolute member need to **START** doing to be a better disciple of Jesus Christ?

BIBLE READING & STUDY TOOLS

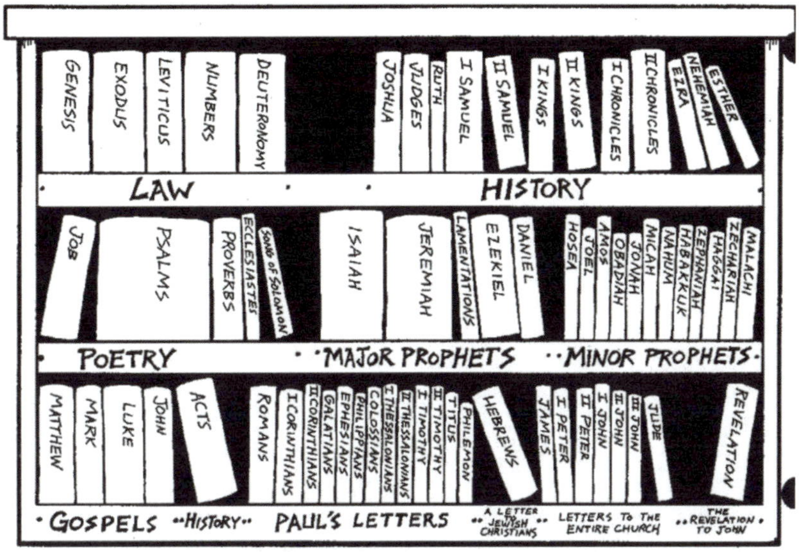

THE OLD TESTAMENT

LAW

GENESIS: The Election of God.
EXODUS: The Redemption of God.
LEVITICUS: The Holiness of God.
NUMBERS: The Faithfulness of God.
DEUTERONOMY: Obedience to God.

HISTORY

JOSHUA: Possession of the Land.
JUDGES: The Book of Apostasy.
RUTH: Redemption by a Kinsman.
1 SAMUEL: Establishment of the Kingdom.
2 SAMUEL: Expansion of the Kingdom.
1 KINGS: Division of the Kingdom.
2 KINGS: Destruction of the Kingdom.
1 CHRONICLES: Preparing for the Temple.
2 CHRONICLES: Building of the Temple.
EZRA: The Book of Restoration.
NEHEMIAH: The Book of Continual Restoration.
ESTHER: The Providence of God.

POETRY

JOB: Suffering of the Righteous.
PSALMS: The Book of Praise.
PROVERBS: The Book of Wisdom.
ECCLESIASTES: The Book of the Futility of Life.
SONG OF SOLOMON: The Book of Love.

SMALL GROUP DISCUSSION:

- Check in or introduce yourself.
- Share one major takeaway or improvement you've experienced over the previous three weeks. What was impacting and why?
- So the Bible is often intimidating to everyone, but share how it intimidates you. Be open and honest

Old Testament Continued: MAJOR PROPHETS

ISAIAH: The Salvation of God.
JEREMIAH: The Judgment of God.
LAMENTATIONS: The Lament.
EZEKIEL: The Glory of God.
DANIEL: The Sovereignty of God.

MINOR PROPHETS

HOSEA: The Love of God.
JOEL: The Day of the Lord.
AMOS: The Judgment of God.
OBADIAH: Judgment on Edom.
JONAH: The Grace of God.
MICAH: Summons to Judgment.
NAHUM: Judgment on Nineveh.
HABAKKUK: The Righteousness of God.
ZEPHANIAH: The Day of the Lord.
HAGGAI: Rebuilding the Temple.
ZECHARIAH: The Future of Jerusalem.
MALACHI: The Charges of God.

THE NEW TESTAMENT GOSPELS

MATTHEW: The Kingship of Jesus Christ.
MARK: The Servanthood of Jesus Christ.
LUKE: The Humanity of Jesus Christ.
JOHN: The Deity of Jesus Christ.

HISTORY

ACTS: The Spread of Christianity.

PAUL'S LETTERS

ROMANS: The Righteousness of God.
1 CORINTHIANS: Disorders in the Church.
2 CORINTHIANS: True Ministry.
GALATIANS: Freedom from the Mosaic Law.
EPHESIANS: Calling of the Believer.

New Testament Continued: PAUL'S LETTERS

PHILIPPIANS: Living Worthy of the Gospel.
COLOSSIANS: The Sufficiency of Christ.
1 THESSALONIANS: The Book of Sanctification.
2 THESSALONIANS: The Book of the Correction of Prophecy.
1 TIMOTHY: Conduct of the Church.
2 TIMOTHY: Ministry of the Word.
TITUS: Order in the Church.
PHILEMON: Example of Love.

LETTER TO HEBREW DISCIPLES

HEBREWS: The Superiority of Christ

LETTERS TO CHURCHES

JAMES: Handling Trials.
1 PETER: Salvation of the Soul.
2 PETER: The Second Coming of Christ.
1 JOHN: Fellowship with the True God.
2 JOHN: The Truth of God.
3 JOHN: The Practice of Love.
JUDE: The Book of False Teachers.

PROPHECY

REVELATION: Judgment by Jesus Christ.

BIBLE STUDY HELPS

BIBLE COMMENTARY – BEST FOR THE COMMON MAN

Written by recognized and popular theologians, commentaries aid in the study of Scripture by providing explanation and interpretation of biblical text. Whether you are just beginning to read Scripture or a student of the Bible, commentaries offer greater understanding with background information on authorship, history, setting, and theme. Commentaries often exposit the New and Old Testament verse by verse.

BIBLE LEXICON – BETTER FOR DEEPER STUDY

Bible lexicons provide definitions and meaning of biblical words found in the original Old Testament Hebrew and New Testament Greek languages. This study resource aids understanding of the origins and root meaning of the ancient languages. Additionally, lexicons explain the cultural context and intended meaning of the original text's author.

BIBLE CONCORDANCE – BETTER FOR DEEPER STUDY

Bible Concordances (especially the *Strong's Exhaustive Concordance*) are complete and easy to use for study notes of the original languages. Combining the text with the power of the Greek and Hebrew lexicons, any student or pastor will enrich his study using these tools.

BIBLE DICTIONARY – BETTER FOR DEEPER STUDY

Bible dictionaries are one of the most practical and useful theological reference tools available. The combination of definitions with online verse reference allows users to easily define and analyze Scripture. Refer to this reference tool in order to discover the meaning of words as well as study them in context to the theological concepts of that specific verse or passage. Popular dictionaries of the Bible include *Baker's Evangelical, Easton's,* and *Smith's* – named after their well-known theological authors.

BIBLE ENCYCLOPEDIA – GOOD FOR ADDITIONAL CONTEXT

Bible encyclopedias contain articles as well as definitions to thousands of words and terms used in Scripture. Entries include full historical references such as date, religious environment, family life, customs, language, and literature. In order to aid a comprehensive understanding of scriptural text, encyclopedias cross reference terms, linking them to the verses where they are found in Scripture. Online articles, written by well-known and respected Christian leaders, help those seeking a greater knowledge of characters, events, and places.

APOCRYPHAL BOOKS – AWARENESS ONLY

These texts are books included as part of the Septuagint (the Greek version of the Old Testament), but not included in the Hebrew Bible. The Roman Catholic and Orthodox churches include all of the Apocrypha (except the books of Esdras and the Prayer of Manasseh), but refer to them as "deuterocanonical" books. Protestant Bibles do not include the Apocrypha, but all of them can be found online for your reading pleasure. Once you read one you will immediately understand why they are not included.

COMPARING TRANSLATIONS

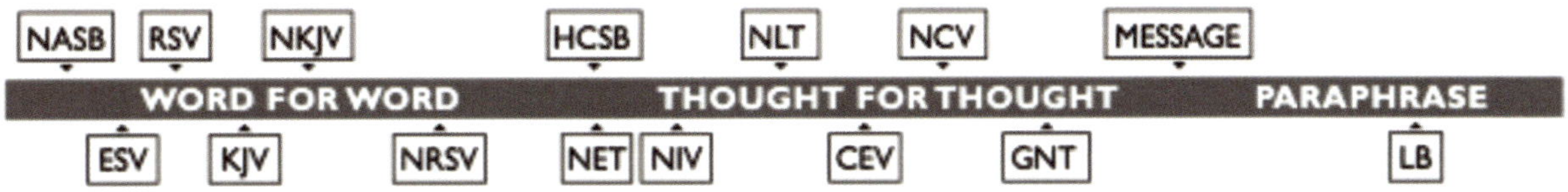

WORD FOR WORD (Formal Equivalent)

Strengths:

- Greater reliance solely on the text.
- Little interpretation of original text.
- Good for in-depth study.
- More precise, though contains complex vocabulary and theological terminology.

Weaknesses:

- Awkward English so potentially less readable.
- Requires more interpretation from the reader.
- Potentially difficult for children and youth, non-Christian or new Christians to read and comprehend.
- Allows the likelihood of readers reaching incorrect interpretive conclusions.

THOUGHT FOR THOUGHT (Functional Equivalent)

Strengths:

- Greater readability.
- Convey meaning over absolute translation so provides less ambiguity.
- Good for public reading.
- Trained scholars interpret the text (as opposed to the casual reader).

Weaknesses:

- Less direct work from the original text.
- Not as beneficial for careful word study.
- Often longer because of the need to explain a technical term using a phrase.

TEXT SAMPLING: GENESIS 28:14

NASB – In you and in your descendants shall all the families of the earth be blessed.
ESV - In you and your offspring shall all the families of the earth be blessed.
RSV - By you and your descendants shall all the families of the earth bless themselves.
KJV - In thee and in thy seed shall all the families of the earth be blessed.
NKJV - In you and in your seed all the families of the earth shall be blessed.
NRSV - All the families of the earth shall be blessed in you and in your offspring.
NIV - All peoples on earth will be blessed through you and your offspring.
CEV - Your family will be a blessing to all people.
MSG - All the families of the Earth will bless themselves in you and your descendants.
LB - And all the nations of the earth will be blessed through you and your descendants.

GENERAL FACTS ON THE BIBLE:

God inspired more than 40 individuals to write the Bible over a time span of nearly 2000 years.

The word "Bible" is derived from the Greek word "biblia" meaning "book." The word "biblia" gets its roots from the word "byblos" meaning "papyrus." Papyrus was the material used for text at that time. The ancient Greeks obtained their supplies of paper (papyrus) from the port of Byblos, located in modern day Lebanon.

The Old Testament contains 39 books; the New Testament contains 27. In total, the Bible includes 66 divinely inspired books.

The Bible includes two testaments known as the Old and New Testament. The word "testament" means "will," "covenant," or "agreement." The Old Testament contains and demonstrates God's promise. The New Testament His fulfillment of the covenant of grace and salvation. These two testaments form the complete book known as the Christian Holy Bible.

The terms "Old Testament" and "New Testament" originated with the prophet Jeremiah. When Jeremiah referenced Israel's future, he proclaimed God would *"make a new covenant with the house of Israel."* Jesus of Nazareth, the long-awaited Messiah, made that new covenant with God's people. The books of the New Testament provide the fulfillment of the promises made throughout the Old Testament.

EVEN MORE FACTS:

- Moses contributed 5 books of the Old Testament.
- Paul contributed 14 books of the New Testament.
- Job is the oldest book of Old Testament written in 1500 B.C.
- Psalm 119 is the longest chapter in the entire Bible.
- The Bible was canonized in. 375.
- The Bible was the first book ever printed in 1454.
- The Holy Bible is the best-selling book of all time sold at a rate of 68,000/day.

The Old Testament was originally written in the Hebrew language, with a few verses or portions of Jeremiah, Daniel, and Ezra written in Aramaic (a dialect developed during the Jewish captivity that gradually took the place of Hebrew as the common language of the Jewish people). The New Testament was originally written in Greek.

The Jewish Bible is the equivalent of our Old Testament.

Under Ptolemy rule, the Hebrew Scriptures were translated into the "Koine" Greek dialect. The translation, an outstanding literary accomplishment, is called the Septuagint. Ptolemy II Philadelphus sponsored the translation project around the third century B.C. According to tradition, 72 Jewish scholars (six from each of the twelve tribes) were summoned for the project and the work was completed in 72 days.

Most Jews of Jesus' day spoke Aramaic, a commonly spoken Syrian language similar to Hebrew. It is not known if Jesus spoke Greek as he left no personal writings.

No doubt Jesus studied the formal Hebrew of the Torah, Prophets, and Writings (Old Testament) because Jewish boys diligently studied theses texts. By the age of 12, Jesus would have been able to recite them by heart. He would have learned by rote from scrolls kept by local teachers or rabbis.

There are more than 24,000 partial and complete manuscript copies of the New Testament. These ancient manuscript copies are public.

BIBLE CANONIZATION

50-100 A.D.: Writing of the New Testament.

140 A.D.: Marcion, an influential businessman in Rome, taught the heresy of two gods: "Yahweh," the cruel god of the Old Testament, and "Abba," the kind father of the New Testament. Marcion eliminated the Old Testament scriptures and since he was anti-Semitic, kept only 10 letters of Paul and 2/3 of Luke's gospel (he deleted references to Jesus' Jewishness). Marcion's false New Testament, the first to be compiled, forced the Church to decide on a core canon. That original canon included the four Gospels and Letters of Paul.

200 A.D.: The periphery of the canon is not yet determined. According to one list compiled in Rome (The Muratorian Canon) the New Testament consisted of the four gospels, Acts, 13 letters of Paul, three of the seven General Epistles (1 John, 2 John, and Jude); and what's known as the Apocalypse of Peter.

367 A.D.: The earliest extant list of the books of the New Testament, in exactly the number and order we have today, is written by St. Athanasius, Bishop of Alexandria.

382 A.D.: Council of Rome meets where Pope Damasus starts the process of defining a universal canon for the Church. The New Testament books are listed in their present number and order.

393 A.D.: At the Council of Hippo, leaders argue, St. Athanasius proposes his Canon.

397 A.D.: The Council of Carthage refines the Canon, sending it to Pope Innocent for ratification. In the East, the canonical process is hampered by a number of schisms (especially within the Church of Antioch).

787 A.D.: The Ecumenical Council of Nicaea II adopts the Canon of Carthage. At this point, both the Latin West and the Greek-Byzantine East hold the same canon. However, the non-Greek Monophysite and Nestorian Churches of the East (the Copts, the Ethiopians, the Syrians, the Armenians, the Syro-Malankars, the Chaldeans, and the Malabars) still didn't agree. These Churches joined in agreement, in 1442 A.D. in Florence.

1227 A.D.: Bible divided into chapters by Stephen Langton, Archbishop of Canterbury. The chapters were divided into verses at a later date.

1442 A.D.: At the Council of Florence the entire Church recognized the 27 books. This council confirmed the Roman Catholic Canon of the Bible which Pope Damasus I had published a thousand years earlier. By 1439, 100 years before the Reformation, all orthodox branches of the Church were legally bound to the same canon.

1536 A.D.: In his translation of the Bible from Greek into German, Luther removed four New Testament books (Hebrews, James, Jude, and Revelation) and placed them in an appendix.

1546 A.D.: At the Council of Trent, the Catholic Church reaffirmed once and for all the complete canon. The council also confirmed the inclusion of the deuterocanonical books which had been a part of the biblical canon since the early Church and was confirmed at the councils of 393 AD, 373, 787 and 1442 AD.

1550 A.D.: Bible divided into verses by Robert Estienne (aka Robert Stephens), a Parisian printer.

SKILL DEVELOPMENT // TIME WITH GOD

Try out your time and location 2 times this week to see how it works for you. (Note: we will be giving ideas for your time, but for now, spend some time in prayer about whatever is on your heart and mind.)

READ: Romans 1-2
MEMORIZE: Romans 3:23

RESOLUTE

INDUCTIVE BIBLE STUDY WORKSHEET

PRAYER/SCRIPTURE TEXT: Write it out here.

OBSERVATIONS

GENRE (circle): Poetry Prose Letter Prophecy Narrative Law History Gospel

MOOD/TONE:

SUBJECT:

VERBS:

STRUCTURE/TRANSITIONS/CONTEXT:

REPEATED WORDS/CONTRASTS/ETC:

INTERPRETATION

OVERARCHING THEME(S):

WHO:

WHAT:

WHEN:

WHERE:

HOW:

APPLICATION

KEY TAKEAWAY: How should I apply?

IMPACT TO RELATIONSHIPS: How should I treat others?

PERSONAL CHANGE: Is there something to repent?

PRAYER

QUOTES

"The great people of the earth today are the people who pray. I do not mean those who talk about prayer, but I mean those people who take time to pray. They have not time. It must be taken from something else. This something else is important, very important and pressing, but still less important and less pressing than prayer."

S.D. Gordon

"If I fail to spend two hours in prayer each morning, the devil gets the victory through the day. I have so much business I cannot get on without spending three hours daily in prayer."

Martin Luther

"Someone once said about Charles Wesley: 'He thought prayer to be more his business than anything else, and I have seen him come out of his closet with a serenity of face next to shining'."

Friend of Charles Wesley

SMALL GROUP DISCUSSION:

- If not already acquainted, introduce yourself.
- What typifies your prayer life or prayer pattern? (For example: how often do you pray, what do you typically pray about, what time of day do you pray).
- If you could change anything about your prayer life what would you change?
- What is the biggest prayer you have ever prayed and the greatest answer you have ever received?
- What would you ask for prayer about currently in your life?
- Take time to pray with and for each other.

THE LORD'S PRAYER

5 "And when you pray, you must not be like the hypocrites. For they love to stand and pray in
the synagogues and at the street corners, that they may be seen by others. Truly, I say to you,
they have received their reward. 6 But when you pray, go into your room and shut the door
and pray to your Father who is in secret. And your Father who sees in secret will reward you.

7 "And when you pray, do not heap up empty phrases as the Gentiles do, for they think that
they will be heard for their many words. 8 Do not be like them, for your Father knows what you
need before you ask him. 9 Pray then like this:

"Our Father in heaven, hallowed be your name.
10 Your kingdom come, your will be done, on earth as it is in heaven.
11 Give us this day our daily bread,
12 and forgive us our debts, as we also have forgiven our debtors.
13 And lead us not into temptation, but deliver us from evil.
14 For if you forgive others their trespasses, your heavenly Father will also forgive you, 15 but if
you do not forgive others their trespasses, neither will your Father forgive your trespasses.

MATTHEW 6:5-15 ESV

THE A.C.T.S. METHOD OF PRAYER

ADORATION: Adoration means worship or spending time adoring and praising God for His attributes and actions. Praise Him for who He is and for all He has done for you. God enjoys hearing our praise.

- "Praise be to God!" Psalm 68:35
- "Praise the Lord! Praise the Lord, O my soul! I will praise the Lord as long as I live; I will sing praises to my God while I have my being." Psalm 146:1

CONFESSION: Agree with God about your wrong attitudes and actions. Express sorrow and regret for what you have said, thought, or done that is not pleasing to Him. Pour out your regrets, seeking God's forgiveness. Know and believe in His forgiveness even when you don't feel it. When you confess your sins, you receive God's forgiveness and cleansing. This action ushers in a humble stance as well as gratitude that removes any barriers blocking your communication with our merciful, loving God.

- "If we confess our sins, He is faithful and just, and will forgive us our sins and purify us from all unrighteousness." 1 John 1:9
- "Whoever conceals his transgressions will not prosper, but he who confesses and forsakes them will obtain mercy." Proverbs 28:13
- "Have mercy on me, O God, according to your steadfast love; according to your abundant mercy blot out my transgressions. Wash me thoroughly from my iniquity, and cleanse me from my sin!" Psalm 51:1-2

THANKSGIVING: Express gratitude to God. Thank Him for His love, protection, and provision. Exercise a stance of gratitude to the One who gives all good gifts.

- "Glorify him with thanksgiving." Psalm 69:30
- "I will offer to you the sacrifice of thanksgiving and call on the name of the Lord." Psalm 116:17

SUPPLICATION: Pray for your needs and the needs of others—your family, friends, pastor, leaders, missionaries, government leaders, and persecuted Christians around the world. Ask for wisdom in every area of your life as well as for His daily guidance, courage, hope, and opportunities to serve.

- "Make your requests known to God." Philippians 4:6
- "Ask, and it will be given to you; seek, and you will find; knock, and it will be opened to you. 8 For everyone who asks receives, and the one who seeks finds, and to the one who knocks it will be opened. 9 Or which one of you, if his son asks him for bread, will give him a stone? 10 Or if he asks for a fish, will give him a serpent? 11 If you then, who are evil, know how to give good gifts to your children, how much more will your Father who is in heaven give good things to those who ask him!" Matthew 7:7-11

MY ACTION ITEMS:

Issues to Address. Steps to Take.

READ: ROMANS 3-4

SKILL DEVELOPMENT // PRAYER

Use the ACTS method of prayer at least twice this week during your time with God.

FEAR & FAITH

SMALL GROUP DISCUSSION:

- Introduce yourself if not already acquainted.
- Over the last few weeks, what theme(s) or issue(s) consumed your mental energy? Describe the situation(s).
- How would you define **fear**? Write out your personal definition and share it with the group.

INDUCTIVE STUDY

JESUS WALKS ON WATER

22 Immediately he made the disciples get into the boat and go before him to the other side,
while he dismissed the crowds. 23 And after he had dismissed the crowds, he went up on the
mountain by himself to pray. When evening came, he was there alone, 24 but the boat by this
time was a long way from the land, beaten by the waves, for the wind was against them. 25
And in the fourth watch of the night he came to them, walking on the sea. 26 But when the disciples saw him walking on the sea, they were terrified, and said, "It is a ghost!" and they cried
out in fear. 27 But immediately Jesus spoke to them, saying, "Take heart; it is I. Do not be
afraid."

28 And Peter answered him, "Lord, if it is you, command me to come to you on the water." 29
He said, "Come." So Peter got out of the boat and walked on the water and came to Jesus. 30
But when he saw the wind, he was afraid, and beginning to sink he cried out, "Lord, save me."
31 Jesus immediately reached out his hand and took hold of him, saying to him, "O you of little
faith, why did you doubt?" 32 And when they got into the boat, the wind ceased. 33 And those
in the boat worshiped him, saying, "Truly you are the Son of God."

MATTHEW 14:22-33

QUOTES:

"The fear of the Lord is the beginning of knowledge." **PROVERBS 1:7**

"The only God ordained fear is the fear of God, and if we fear Him, we don't have to fear anyone or anything else." **MARK BATTERSON**

"The only thing we have to fear is fear itself." **FRANKLIN DELANO ROOSEVELT**

Fear is to "feel wonder and a certain shrinking." **C. S. LEWIS**

"I have learned over the years that when one's mind is made up; this diminishes fear; knowing what must be done does away with fear." **ROSA PARKS**

"One of the greatest discoveries a man makes, one of his great surprises, is to find he can do what he was afraid he couldn't do." **HENRY FORD**

This is called the "Jesus Boat." Discovered by, Moshe and Yuval Lufan, brothers and fishermen who discovered the Ancient Galilee Boat in 1986, buried in the mud near the shore of the Sea of Galilee.

MY ACTION ITEMS:

Issues to Address. Steps to Take.

What fear do I need to address? What step am I going to take to transform this into holy fear?

READ: Romans 4-5
MEMORIZE: Romans 6:23

SMALL GROUP DISCUSSION:

- If you had been in the boat and Jesus asked you to step out, what would you have done?
- What decision(s) do you need to make right now in order to fight fear in your life?
- Spiritually speaking, in what area of your life do you sense Jesus inviting you to step out in?
- Why is He inviting you to step out in faith?

SKILL DEVELOPMENT // PRAYER

Using the ACTS method, try 2 of the following 3 types of prayer (on 2 different days): write your prayers; pray while taking a walk; and/or pray while driving.

SIN

SMALL GROUP DISCUSSION:

- Check in with each other.
- As a kid, what is the dumbest thing you did?
- What is the most prevalent sin (or sins) you see taking down men in the home, work, or in churches today? Why?
- What impact does this have?

THE TEMPTATION

1 Now the serpent was more crafty than any other beast of the field that the Lord God had
made. He said to the woman, "Did God actually say, 'You shall not eat of any tree in the garden'?" 2 And the woman said to the serpent, "We may eat of the fruit of the trees in the garden, 3 but God said, 'You shall not eat of the fruit of the tree that is in the midst of the garden,
neither shall you touch it, lest you die.'" 4 But the serpent said to the woman, "You will not
surely die. 5 For God knows that when you eat of it your eyes will be opened, and you will be
like God, knowing good and evil." 6 So when the woman saw that the tree was good for food,
and that it was a delight to the eyes, and that the tree was to be desired to make one wise,
she took of its fruit and ate, and she also gave some to her husband who was with her, and he
ate. 7 Then the eyes of both were opened, and they knew that they were naked. And they
sewed fig leaves together and made themselves loincloths. 8 And they heard the sound of the
Lord God walking in the garden in the cool of the day, and the man and his wife hid themselves from the presence of the Lord God among the trees of the garden. 9 But the Lord God
called to the man and said to him, "Where are you?" 10 And he said, "I heard the sound of you
in the garden, and I was afraid, because I was naked, and I hid myself." 11 He said, "Who told
you that you were naked? Have you eaten of the tree of which I commanded you not to eat?"
12 The man said, "The woman whom you gave to be with me, she gave me fruit of the tree,
and I ate." 13 Then the Lord God said to the woman, "What is this that you have done?" The
woman said, "The serpent deceived me, and I ate."

14 The Lord God said to the serpent, "Because you have done this, cursed are you above all
livestock and above all beasts of the field; on your belly you shall go, and dust you shall eat all
the days of your life. 15 I will put enmity between you and the woman, and between your offspring and her offspring; he shall bruise your head, and you shall bruise his heel."

16 To the woman he said, "I will surely multiply your pain in childbearing; in pain you shall bring
forth children. Your desire shall be for your husband, and he shall rule over you."

17 And to Adam he said, "Because you have listened to the voice of your wife and have eaten
of the tree of which I commanded you, 'You shall not eat of it,' cursed is the ground because
of you; in pain you shall eat of it all the days of your life; 18 thorns and thistles it shall bring
forth for you; and you shall eat the plants of the field. 19 By the sweat of your face you shall
eat bread, till you return to the ground, for out of it you were taken; for you are dust, and to
dust you shall return."

20 The man called his wife's name Eve, because she was the mother of all living. 21 And the
Lord God made for Adam and for his wife garments of skins and clothed them.

22 Then the Lord God said, "Behold, the man has become like one of us in knowing good and
evil. Now, lest he reach out his hand and take also of the tree of life and eat, and live forever—"
23 therefore the Lord God sent him out from the garden of Eden to work the ground from
which he was taken. 24 He drove out the man, and at the east of the Garden of Eden he
placed the cherubim and a flaming sword that turned every way to guard the way to the tree
of life.

GENESIS 3

TAKE IT FURTHER

GOD | GENESIS 2:16-17

"And the Lord God commanded the man, saying, "You may surely eat of every tree of the garden, but of the tree of the knowledge of good and evil you shall not eat, for in the day that you eat of it you shall surely die."

SATAN | GENESIS 3:1

"Did God actually say, 'You shall not eat of any tree in the garden'?"

EVE | GENESIS 3:2-3

"We may eat of the fruit of the trees in the garden, but God said, 'You shall not eat of the fruit of the tree that is in the midst of the garden, neither shall you touch it, lest you die.'"

- *Compare the verses and uncover the lie, temptation, and/or trickery.*

GOD | GENESIS 2:16-17

"And the Lord God commanded the man, saying, "You may surely eat of every tree of the garden, but of the tree of the knowledge of good and evil you shall not eat, for in the day that you eat of it you shall surely die."

SATAN | GENESIS 3:4-5

"You will not surely die. For God knows that when you eat of it your eyes will be opened, and you will be like God, knowing good and evil."

EVE | GENESIS 3:6

So when the woman saw that the tree was good for food, and that it was a delight to the eyes, and that the tree was to be desired to make one wise, she took of its fruit and ate, and she also gave some to her husband who was with her, and he ate.

- *What lie, temptation, and/or trickery are found in these verses?*

MY ACTION ITEMS:

Issues to Address. Steps to Take.

What sin do you need to address? What steps are you going to take to address this sin?

SKILL DEVELOPMENT // PRAYER

During one or more prayer times this week think through the events of the previous day. Pay attention to any high or low points of the day and pray about them as a part of your prayer time that day. Use the ACTS method on other days.

READ: ROMANS 7-8

REPENTANCE

SMALL GROUP DISCUSSION:

- Check in with each other.
- Identify one behavior of your employer, a coworker, and if you dare, your spouse that you would love to see changed. Explain why you desire the change. Explain how the objectionable behavior impacts you.
- Can you recall the last time you heard a politician say "I'm sorry?" Why is admitting failure or wrong doing so hard?
- What have been the hardest thoughts, behaviors, and/or attitudes for you to change in your life thus far?
- How would you define "repentance?" Write out your definition.

"From that time Jesus began to preach, saying, 'Repent, for the kingdom of heaven is at hand.'"

MATTHEW 4:17

"In those days John the Baptist came preaching in the wilderness of Judea, 'Repent, for the kingdom of heaven is at hand.'"

MATTHEW 3:1-2

"If my people who are called by my name humble themselves, and pray and seek my face and turn from their wicked ways, then I will hear from heaven and will forgive their sin and heal their land."

2 CHRONICLES 7:14

RESOLUTE

REPENTANCE DEFINED:

In biblical Greek, metanoeō (μετανοέω) and metanoia (μετάνοια) denote a *"change of mind, sorrow, and an about face in action of the whole inner nature, intellectual, affectional, and moral."*

FOUR QUALITIES (FRUIT) OF GENUINE REPENTANCE:

Here are four qualities of genuine repentance:

- Mental **awareness** of need for a change.
- Emotional **sorrow** for impact to God/others.
- Changed **action** from old behavior to new.
- Sincere **motivation** for the change.

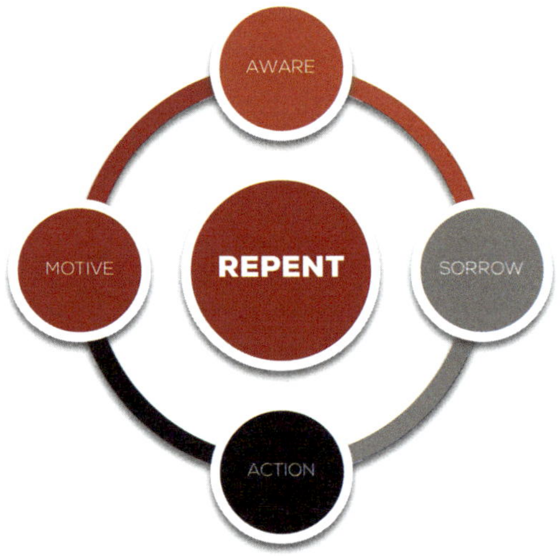

THE PRODIGAL SON AND THE FORGIVING FATHER

In the well-known Biblical story of The Prodigal Son we see all four of these qualities present in the younger son. While they appear to be in a sequential order, the qualities occur more randomly and instantaneously rather than sequentially. Yet they give us a good example of genuine repentance. Notice the qualities in the text.

"But when he **came to himself** (Aware), he said, 'How many of my father's hired servants have more than enough bread, but I perish here with hunger! **I will arise and go** (Action) to my father, and I will say to him, "Father, **I have sinned against heaven and before you** (Motive/Sorrow). **I am no longer worthy** (Sorrow) to be called your son. **Treat me as one of your hired servants**. (Motives)"'

LUKE 15:17-19

MY ACTION ITEMS:

Issues to Address. Steps to Take.

What do you need to repent of? What steps are you going to today?

SMALL GROUP DISCUSSION:

- Which of the *counterfeit repentances* are you most prone to use?
- Do you require a *mental, emotional or behavioral* breakthrough in order to enter into genuine repentance?
- Is there something you need to repent of today?
- Determine a method for holding one another accountable this week.

FOUR TYPES OF COUNTERFEIT REPENTANCE:

TYPE ONE: DEFENSIVENESS, EXPLAINING, OR BLAMING

Assigning responsibility for your actions to someone else because the heart is unauthentic or unreceptive. This can include minimizing the issue by detailing the facts.

"He said, 'Who told you that you were naked? Have you eaten of the tree of which I commanded you not to eat?' The man said, 'The woman whom you gave to be with me, she gave me fruit of the tree, and I ate.' Then the Lord God said to the woman, 'What is this that you have done?' The woman said, 'The serpent deceived me, and I ate.'" Genesis 3:11-13

HOW OFTEN DO YOU DO THIS?

LOW 1 2 3 4 5 6 7 8 9 10 HIGH

TYPE TWO: REGRET

Feeling bad about a sin while being unwilling to make action or attitude adjustments.

"For the sorrow that is according to the will of God produces a repentance without regret, leading to salvation; but the sorrow of the world produces death." 2 Corinthians 7:10

HOW OFTEN DO YOU DO THIS?

LOW 1 2 3 4 5 6 7 8 9 10 HIGH

TYPE THREE: CONDITIONAL REPENTANCE

An apology made in hope of alieving pain while masking genuine motivation because they are manipulating or expecting something in return. Often seeking the path of least resistance from pain or discomfort.

"Then Pharaoh sent and called Moses and Aaron and said to them, 'This time I have sinned; the LORD is in the right, and I and my people are in the wrong.'" Exodus 9:27

HOW OFTEN DO YOU DO THIS?

LOW 1 2 3 4 5 6 7 8 9 10 HIGH

TYPE FOUR: ENGINEERED REPENTANCE

Pretending to save face and/or an attempt to look good to others; pure manipulation.

"Two men went up into the temple to pray, one a Pharisee and the other a tax collector. The Pharisee, standing by himself, prayed thus: 'God, I thank you that I am not like other men, extortioners, unjust, adulterers, or even like this tax collector. I fast twice a week; I give tithes of all that I get.' But the tax collector, standing far off, would not even lift up his eyes to heaven, but beat his breast, saying, 'God, be merciful to me, a sinner!'" Luke 18:10-14

HOW OFTEN DO YOU DO THIS?

LOW 1 2 3 4 5 6 7 8 9 10 HIGH

READ: Romans 9-10
MEMORIZE: Romans 5:8

SKILL DEVELOPMENT // PRAYER

During one or more prayer times think through the previous day and reflect on the high and low points of the day. Pay particular attention to any situations that might lead you to confession. Take time to confess and sincerely repent around this situation and any broader patterns of sin related to it. If nothing comes to mind, think back over the previous few days.

MILESTONES

SAMUEL JUDGES ISRAEL

3 And Samuel said to all the house of Israel, "If you are
returning to the Lord with all your heart, then put away
the foreign gods and the Ashtaroth from among you
and direct your heart to the Lord and serve him only,
and he will deliver you out of the hand of the Philistines."
4 So the people of Israel put away the Baals and the
Ashtaroth, and they served the Lord only.

5 Then Samuel said, "Gather all Israel at Mizpah, and I
will pray to the Lord for you." 6 So they gathered at
Mizpah and drew water and poured it out before the
Lord and fasted on that day and said there, "We have
sinned against the Lord." And Samuel judged the people of Israel at Mizpah. 7 Now when the Philistines heard
that the people of Israel had gathered at Mizpah, the
lords of the Philistines went up against Israel. And when
the people of Israel heard of it, they were afraid of the
Philistines. 8 And the people of Israel said to Samuel,
"Do not cease to cry out to the Lord our God for us, that
he may save us from the hand of the Philistines." 9 So
Samuel took a nursing lamb and offered it as a whole
burnt offering to the Lord. And Samuel cried out to the
Lord for Israel, and the Lord answered him. 10 As Samuel was offering up the burnt offering, the Philistines
drew near to attack Israel. But the Lord thundered with a mighty sound that day against the
Philistines and threw them into confusion, and they were defeated before Israel. 11 And the
men of Israel went out from Mizpah and pursued the Philistines and struck them, as far as below Beth-car.

12 Then Samuel took a stone and set it up between Mizpah and Shen and called its name
Ebenezer; for he said, "Till now the Lord has helped us." 13 So the Philistines were subdued and
did not again enter the territory of Israel. And the hand of the Lord was against the Philistines
all the days of Samuel. 14 The cities that the Philistines had taken from Israel were restored to
Israel, from Ekron to Gath, and Israel delivered their territory from the hand of the Philistines.
There was peace also between Israel and the Amorites.

1 SAMUEL 7:3-14

COME THOU FOUNT OF EVERY BLESSING

"Here I raise my Ebenezer; Hither by Thy help I've come;"

SAMUEL JOHNSON, Author

"People need to be reminded more often than they need to be instructed."

RESOLUTE

MILESTONES ON YOUR TIMELINE

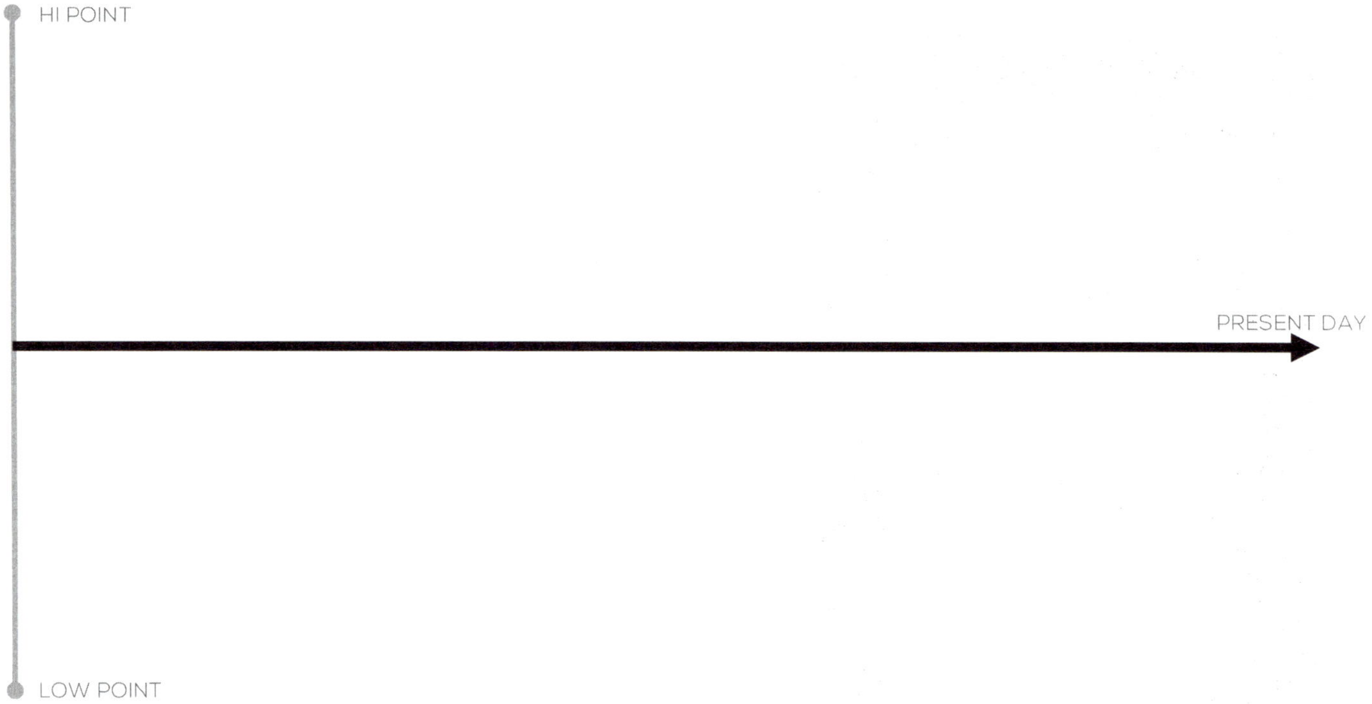

Use the following to identify milestones that carry significance to you. The beginning of the line represents your birth and the ending arrow represents present day. Use key words as markers.

- **MAJOR LIFE EVENTS**: Marriage, divorce, first home, college years, graduate school, child's birth, or bankruptcy.
- **MAJOR LIFE SITUATIONS**: Death of loved one, sin issue, family struggles, accidents or physical injuries.
- **SIGNIFICANT CAREER CHANGES OR CHALLENGES**: Jobs, career changes, new business launch, career advancements, layoffs, or scandals at work.
- **PLACES YOU HAVE LIVED AND HOW THEY ALTERED YOU**. Locations, customs, cultures, languages, practices.
- **SIGNIFICANT SPIRITUAL RELATIONSHIPS OR MAJOR SPIRITUAL MOMENTS**: A person, conversation, theological moment, lesson or sermon, practices, mission trip, a church debate or issue.
- Mark the following with these images:
  - The Moment You Made a Profession of Faith. Mark with a ✝.
  - The Moment You Were Baptized. Mark with a **B**.
  - Moments You Experienced Deep Spiritual Growth: Mark with an ↑.

READ: ROMANS 11-12

BIBLICAL CHARACTERS & THEIR MILESTONES:

The Milestones of Samuel:

- The location of the battle was Ebenezer (1 Samuel 4:1-11).
- The moving of the ark from Ebenezer (1 Samuel 5:1-12).
- The final battle at the Ebenezer (1 Samuel 7:2-12).

The Milestones of Moses:

- Twelve standing stones (Exodus 24:2-4).
- The original two Stone Tablets (Exodus 31:12-18).
- The second two Stone Tablets (Exodus 34:1-4).

The Milestones of Joshua:

- The twelve stones of the Jordan (Joshua 4:1-9).
- The large standing stone as a covenant (Joshua 24:14-28).

MY ACTION ITEMS:

Issues to Address. Steps to Take.

How do view your milestones? What steps do you need to take to better understand your story?

IDENTIFYING YOUR STYLE

SMALL GROUP DISCUSSION:

- How often do you share your testimony (milestones from last week) with others?
- Do you consider sharing your faith difficult? If so, why? What situations seem especially difficult? Are there situations where sharing your faith might be easy?
- Why do you suppose Jesus' 12 disciples easily gave all they had for God? What motivated them even to the point of death?
- Have you ever led someone to Christ? If so, share the experience.

RESOLUTE

STYLE ASSESSMENT

Scoring: 3 = Very Often | 2 = Often | 1 = Sometimes | 0 = Not Usually

___ 1. In conversations, I like to approach topics directly without much small talk or beating around the bush.

___ 2. I have a hard time leaving bookstores or online libraries without getting a bunch of books that will help me better understand issues being debated in society.

___ 3. I often tell stories about my personal experiences to illustrate a point I am trying to make.

___ 4. I am a "people person" who places a high value on friendship.

___ 5. I enjoy including or adding new people to activities I am involved in.

___ 6. I see needs in people's lives that others often overlook.

___ 7. I do not shy away from putting a person on the spot when it seems necessary.

___ 8. I tend to be analytical.

___ 9. I often identify with others by using phrases like "I used to think that too" or "I once felt the way you do."

___ 10. Other people have commented on my skill in developing new friendships.

___ 11. To be honest, even if I knew the answers, I would rather have someone better qualified than me explain Christianity to my friends.

___ 12. I find fulfillment in helping others, often in behind-the-scenes ways.

___ 13. I do not have a problem confronting my friends with the truth even if it risks hurting our relationship.

___ 14. In conversations, I naturally focus on the questions holding up a person's spiritual progress.

___ 15. When I tell people how I came to Christ, I have found they have been interested in hearing it.

___ 16. I would rather delve into personal life issues than abstract theological concepts.

___ 17. If I knew of a high-quality outreach event that my friends would enjoy, I would try to bring them.

___ 18. I prefer to show love through my actions more than with words.

___ 19. I believe genuine love often means telling someone the truth, even when it hurts.

___ 20. I enjoy discussion and debate on difficult issues.

___ 21. I intentionally share my mistakes with others when helps them relate to the solutions I have found.

___ 22. I prefer getting involved in discussions concerning a person's life before dealing with the details of his beliefs.

___ 23. I tend to watch for spiritually strategic events to bring people to, like Christian concerts, outreach events, and seeker services.

___ 24. When people are spiritually closed, I have found that my quiet demonstration of Christ-like love sometimes makes them more receptive.

___ 25. A fitting motto for me is: "Make a difference or a mess, but do something."

___ 26. I often get frustrated with people when they use weak arguments or poor logic.

___ 27. People seem interested in hearing stories about things that have happened in my life.

___ 28. I enjoy long talks with friends.

___ 29. I am always looking for a match between the needs and interests of my friends and the various events, books, etc., they would enjoy or benefit from.

___ 30. I feel more comfortable physically assisting a person in the name of Christ over getting involved in religious discussions.

___ 31. I sometimes get in trouble for lacking gentleness and sensitivity in the way I interact with others.

___ 32. I like to get at the underlying reasons for the opinions people hold.

___ 33. I am still amazed at how God brought me to faith in Him and am motivated to tell people about it.

___ 34. People generally consider me an interactive, sensitive, and caring person.

___ 35. A highlight of my week would be to take a guest to an appropriate church event.

___ 36. I tend to be more practical and action oriented than philosophical and idea oriented.

SELF-SCORE ON THE NEXT PAGE...

RESOLUTE

SCORING:

Confronting	Intellectual	Testimonial	Interpersonal	Invitational	Serving
#1 ______	#2 ______	#3 ______	#4 ______	#5 ______	#6 ______
#7 ______	#8 ______	#9 ______	#10 _____	#11 _____	#12 _____
#13 _____	#14 _____	#15 _____	#16 _____	#17 _____	#18 _____
#19 _____	#20 _____	#21 _____	#22 _____	#23 _____	#24 _____
#25 _____	#26 _____	#27 _____	#28 _____	#29 _____	#30 _____
#31 _____	#32 _____	#33 _____	#34 _____	#35 _____	#36 _____
TOTAL	TOTAL	TOTAL	TOTAL	TOTAL	TOTAL
______	______	______	______	______	______

READ: Romans 13-14
MEMORIZE: Romans 10:9

SMALL GROUP QUESTIONS:

- What did you score highest on, and lowest on?
- Read the corresponding descriptions.
- Does this accurately describe you, and your style of leading people to Christ? How effective are you at using this style? How can you improve?
- Let your partner ask you any questions he may have to learn more about your style.

SOME KEYS REGARDLESS OF YOUR STYLE:

MY ACTION ITEMS:

Issues to Address. Steps to Take.

What do I need to know about my style of talking about Christ? What steps do I take to ensure I am communicating the story of Christ effectively?

RESOLUTE

CONFRONTATIONAL STYLE

GENERAL QUALITIES:

- Confident, bold and direct.
- Skips small talk, likes to get right to the point.
- Holds strong opinions and convictions.

INTELLECTUAL STYLE

GENERAL QUALITIES:

- Analytical, logical and inquisitive.
- Likes to debate.
- Concerned with what people think over what they feel.

TESTIMONIAL STYLE

GENERAL QUALITIES:

- Clear communicator and listener.
- Transparent sharing of personal life experiences, both triumphs and difficulties.
- Links own experience to that of others.

INTERPERSONAL STYLE

GENERAL QUALITIES:

- Conversational and sensitive.
- Friendship oriented.
- Focuses on others and their needs.

INVITATIONAL STYLE

GENERAL QUALITIES:

- Enjoys meeting new people.
- Committed, strong belief in commitments.
- Sees outreach events as unique opportunities.

SERVING STYLE

GENERAL QUALITIES:

- Sees needs and finds joy in meeting them.
- Shows love through action more than words.
- Attaches value to even menial tasks.

LEADING TO CHRIST

"But in your hearts honor Christ the Lord as holy, always being prepared to make a defense to anyone who asks you for a reason for the hope that is in you." 1 Peter 3:15.

IDENTIFYING THE SPECTRUM OF BELIEF

RESISTING
• Negative view of Christianity
• It is okay for you but not for me
QUESTIONING
• Realizes there is more to life than what is seen
• Willing to engage in a spiritual conversation
TRUSTING
• Accepts that God is holy and that they are sinful
• Trusts in Jesus as Savior instead of self
GROWING
• Growing spiritually and in community
• Daily practicing repentance and faith
SERVING
• Serving their church, family, work and community
• Actively sharing their story and the gospel
GOING
• Making disciples
• Missionary to the workplace and world

FRAMEWORK FOR THE CONVERSATION

This is meant to guide you through three movements in a spiritual conversation.

__________ STORY

Just simply listen to what has brought them to this point in their life. Listen for both *felt need* and *sin pattern*.

__________ STORY

You do not need to share your whole personal story, but by recalling portions of it, especially your *felt need* and *sin pattern* you will be able to create a connection. Even if you have never been in the other guy's shoes, you have lived in *sin* and struggled with your own *felt need issues* that brought you to the point where you made a profession of faith. Letting him know you connect with his story establishes connection and credibility.

__________ STORY

Human Sin, *God's Love*, *Jesus' Sacrifice and Resurrection*, and the gift of *Eternal Life* are segments of the most beautiful love story ever told. It is a story we need to know and memorize so it flows naturally when we share it.

A CASE STUDY

Read the following and discuss how you might lead this person to Christ. Try to imagine this as a real person and use the methodology we discussed on the last page to lead him toward Christ. Remember to focus on finding his *felt need* and *sin pattern* as you listen.

Dave's Story

Growing up I attended a Catholic church. I'm the youngest in a family with 5 children. I have always felt lost and forgotten, and very insignificant. My relationship with my father is part of the reason I feel so unimportant. I'm also mad at God for making me the way he did because I was an "oops" baby - you know, an unplanned pregnancy. Maybe that's why I felt nothing I did was good enough for my dad. He didn't seem to want me, so I have always wondered how God value me? And therefore, I walked away from the Catholic Church as an act of rebellion when I was a teen.

During my teenage years, I took the easy route of escape in alcohol and drugs. I didn't even try for typical school accomplishments because my parents never noticed when I did succeed. But they sure did notice when I got in trouble or did anything wrong, though. So, I was drawn to reckless behavior – at least then my parents noticed me. My dad and his friends all drank and used drugs to escape life so that became my solution, too. A dependable one for me but my problems with my parents escalated.

In high school, I had some bad experiences. A few times I was the object of ridicule and jokes. So, to fit in, I used girls. Many of my friends told me that I had a drug problem and I hated them for labeling me like that and eventually, I became emotionally numb. I figured if I were numb, then would hurt anymore. So, I kept others at a distance, not letting anyone in. Honestly, I didn't let people in because I was ashamed of myself – who I had become. Eventually, I started considering suicide. The thoughts would come at the weirdest times – more and more often. I felt I had no future.

Then I met a few Christians who became friends. At first I pushed them away, but they kept coming back and I really don't know why. I drank away my issues and didn't want to face God. By then, my father was out of the picture. He didn't change, so it was clear to me that I wouldn't be able to either. God wasn't real to me because when I needed Him in high school, when I thought I believed in Him, He didn't help me. And of course I felt abandoned by God.

Somehow, I've found myself attending church again. I never thought that would happen. I am going because I feel like there is no other place to go. The people at church seem friendly and something keeps drawing me back – maybe it's God. I am talking with you because I see something different in your life. You seem to have things together and trustworthy. I would talk to the Pastor but he probably won't be able to relate to me. Do you have time to talk? I am tired of living this way and I want to make a change.

RESOLUTE

ROMANS ROAD

The book of Romans provides guidance through four major concepts regarding our relationship with God and how we inherit eternal life. The stops on the journey illustrate the concepts of **sin**, the **penalty of sin**, sacrificial **love**, and the **decision** to confess and believe in Christ's redeeming sacrifice. Whenever possible, have a Bible with you to point out the verses, but try to have them memorized. As you read the verses, keep in mind the meaning behind the words that tell His story.

STOP ONE: ROMANS 3:23

"*For all* have *sinned* and fall short of the glory of God."

- *SINNED*: To miss the mark by not living the way God designed us to live and choosing instead to be our own life leader. Most call this living a self-directed life.
- *FOR ALL*: Everyone, every person who has ever lived or will live, without exception.

STOP TWO: ROMANS 6:23

"For the *wages* of sin is *death*."

- *DEATH*: Refers to two types of death; **spiritual** and **physical**. We will all die a physical death. Spiritual death refers to eternal separation from God that results in spending an eternity in hell. Spend some time on this truth as it may be a new concept for some.
- *WAGES*: What we've earned or deserve as payment for our actions. The penalty, or wage earned for our sin is death. That's the bad news. Good news follows, but don't rush there for the discomfort of this hard reality. When handled with humility and respect, people respond well. Be a safe person for others to consider this issue and sit in a discussion of sin without pointing fingers or judging harshly.

STOP THREE: ROMANS 5:8

"*But God shows his love* for us in that while we were still sinners, *Christ died for us*."

- *GOD SHOWS HIS LOVE*: God sees our hopeless position and knows the impossibility of our conquering sin on our own. We have chosen to live apart from God, living a self-directed life. In His vast love and mercy, God has provided our escape. He sent His Son to rescue us from our despair and provide forgiveness. The person you are talking with may be experiencing despair by thinking God will not forgive his sin. Assure him that God forgives all sin past, present, and future for those who believe.
- *CHRIST DIED FOR US*: Jesus, who lived a pure and holy life without sin, stepped in to pay the penalty for us. He died as a sacrifice for our sin. Jesus is God's loving rescue.

STOP FOUR: ROMANS 10:9-10

"Because, if you *confess* with your mouth that *Jesus is Lord* and *believe* in your heart that God *raised him from the dead*, you will be saved. For with the heart one believes and is justified, and with the mouth one confesses and is saved."

- *CONFESS:* We are called to confess the choice we have made to live a self-directed life and confess also the desire to live a God-directed life.
- *JESUS IS LORD*: Saying out loud that we are now choosing to surrender to the Lordship of Jesus Christ means to proclaim a new life leader.
- *BELIEVING*: To know in our heart that God, Jesus, sin, death, and resurrection are real and that He defeated sin in the resurrection.
- *RAISED HIM FROM THE DEAD*: This is the proof that God has the power to defeat both types of death: physical and spiritual.

THE CLOSER

This is the most important question you will ever ask. Here are a few ways to ask it, but you better have this one memorized!

- Are you ready to say yes to Christ?
- Are you ready to make this decision?
- Are you ready to make Jesus Christ your life leader?
- Are you ready to make Jesus Christ your Lord and Savior?

If the individual says "yes," move on to the next step, praying together.

THE PRAYER

Though not directly stated in Scripture, this two-part prayer provides a great way to mark the moment of decision. Some will have no idea how to pray or may have not ever actually prayed before. You can help by leading the prayer. First pray the words yourself, then have the other person repeats the prayer. This format guides the repentant individual who may feel emotional, and insecure in talking to God.

Part One: The personal prayer.

Pray out loud for the individual. Simply follow the first four stops explained above.

Part Two: The repeating prayer.

You pray and the individual repeats after you. The following provides language that may be beneficial.

- **Sin** – "God I have been living my way..."
- **Confess** – "I want to turn from my sin..."
- **Repentance** – "I want to make you my Lord and Savior..."
- **Holy Spirit** – "Holy Spirit come into my life today..."

After completing the prayer, offer congratulations on becoming a part of God's family. Affirm their first step toward a life-changing relationship that will shape and renew the individual's future.

READ: ROMANS 15-16

SKILL DEVELOPMENT // SHARING

During a time with God, ask him to show you those in your life at different parts of the spiritual spectrum and what steps you could take to connect with them given where they are at spiritually.

SUFFICIENCY OF SCRIPTURE

SMALL GROUP QUESTIONS:

- When you are angry, depressed, frustrated, or anxious where do you turn for answers? Be honest, what's your first impulse and where to you go/what do you do?
- Identify and briefly describe the biggest life issue that you struggle with at this time.
- What are your thoughts about that issue?
- In the past, how have you tried to overcome this problem? Have your efforts worked?
- How do you think God views the situation?

READ: Genesis 1:27

Who created man?

READ: Genesis 2:4-7

How much care did God give to creating man?

READ: Psalm 8:3-9

What are the position and qualities of man at the time of creation?

READ: Psalm 139:1-18

What does God know about man? List as many phrases or concepts as possible.

THE PROFIT OF SCRIPTURE

16 "All Scripture is breathed out by God and profitable for teaching, for reproof, for correction,
and for training in righteousness, 17 that the man of God may be complete, equipped for every
good work."

2 TIMOTHY 3:16-17

PROFIT 1 - TEACHING: To ____________ us the path.
PROFIT 2 - REPROOF: To tell us when we get _______________ the path.
PROFIT 3 - CORRECTION: To illustrate how to get _____________ on the path.
PROFIT 4 - TRAINING: To indicate how to __________ on the path.

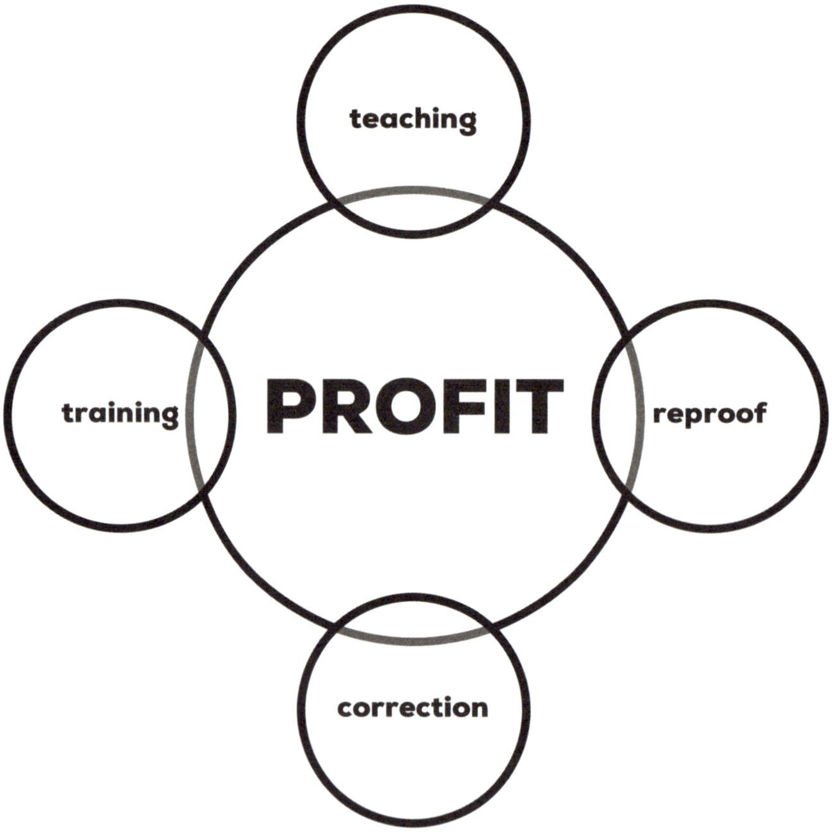

RESOLUTE

COMPLETE & EQUIPPED BY SCRIPTURE

16 "All Scripture is breathed out by God and profitable for teaching, for reproof, for correction, and for training in righteousness, 17 that the man of God may be **complete, equipped** for every good work."

2 TIMOTHY 3:16-17

SCRIPTURE'S HAS UNDENIABLE POWER

"The law of the Lord is perfect, reviving the
soul; the testimony of the Lord is sure,
making wise the simple; 8 the precepts of
the Lord are right, rejoicing the heart; the
commandment of the Lord is pure, enlightening the eyes; 9 the fear of the Lord is
clean, enduring forever; the rules of the
Lord are true, and righteous altogether."

PSALM 19:7-9

"Is not my word like fire, declares the Lord, and like a hammer that breaks the rock in pieces?"

JEREMIAH 23:29

FIVE IMPLICATIONS

"COMPLETE & EQUIPPED DOES & DOES NOT IMPLY…"

1. Implies that it is ________________________ for direction.
2. Implies that it is _____________ we need living a godly life.
3. Implies that we cannot use it as an ____________________.
4. Does not imply we _________________________ scripture.

Does not imply that scripture is _____________________.

MY ACTION ITEMS:

Issues to Address. Steps to Take.

How do you typically address issues in your life – by going to scripture or other people? What steps do you need to take to ensure you are going to scripture first?

SKILL DEVELOPMENT // BIBLE READING

Do an inductive study of Psalms 19:7-11 during one of your times with God. (Write in your Bible or print passage from www.biblegateway.com). After making observations, choose one application and pray about it during your prayer time.